**SELECT
EDITIONS**

Friendship

illustrations.
JAN GALLEHAWK

calligraphy:
JIM BILLINGSLEY

ISBN: 1 86476 012 5

Friendship is love without his wings

Lord George Byron

The only way
to have a
friend is
to be one

Ralph Waldo Emerson

Love demands
infinitely less
than friendship.

George Jean Nathan

THE SEVEREST

TEST OF CHARACTER
IS NOT SO MUCH THE
ABILITY TO KEEP A SECRET
AS IT IS, BUT WHEN THE
SECRET IS FINALLY OUT,
TO REFRAIN FROM DISCLOSING
THAT YOU KNEW IT
ALL ALONG.

The friendship
of a child is
the brightest
gem
set upon
the circlet
of society

Make new friends,
but keep the old;

those are silver.
these are gold.

Joseph Parry

if you think you are beaten, you are;
if you think you dare not, you don't;
if you'd like to win, but think you can't
it's almost a cinch you won't.

if you think you'll lose, you're lost;
for out in the world we find
success begins with a fellow's Will~
it's all in the state of mind.

if you think you are outclassed, you are;
you've got to think high to rise.
you've just got·to·be sure of yourself
before you can win the prize.

life's battles don't always go
to the stronger or faster man,
but sooner or later the man who wins
is the one who thinks he can.

Hold on to your temper
and keep your patience
under all circumstances,
for when you yield to
vengeance you destroy
or retard reconciliation.

NOTHING IS IMPOSSIBLE TO A WILLING HEART.

It is easier to find fault with others, but it is not easy to live so that others will not see faults in us.

We tend to criticise our friends for doing things we could do no better.

Yesterday is but
a reflection

Today is now

Tomorrow
is a bonus.

Jim Billingsley

Choose your friends
with care,

that you may
have choice
friends.

TEN GOOD THINGS:~

THERE ARE TEN GOOD THINGS
FOR WHICH NO MAN HAS EVER
BEEN SORRY:—
FOR DOING GOOD TO ALL ;
FOR SPEAKING EVIL OF NO ONE ;
FOR HEARING BEFORE JUDGING;
FOR THINKING BEFORE SPEAKING;
FOR HOLDING AN ANGRY TONGUE ;
FOR BEING KIND TO THE DISTRESSED;
FOR ASKING PARDON FOR ALL WRONGS;
FOR BEING PATIENT TOWARD EVERYBODY;
FOR STOPPING THE EAR OF TALE BEARER;
FOR DIS-BELIEVING MOST OF THE EVIL REPORTS.

I breathed a song into the air,
It fell to earth, I know not where;
For who has sight so keen and strong,
That it can follow the flight
                              of song:—
The song from beginning to end,
I found again in the heart
                        of a friend.
(Exerpt)

Henry Wadsworth Longfellow

Duty makes us
do things well,

but Love makes
us do them
beautifully.

Rev. Phillip Brooks

True friendship
comes when
silence between
two people
becomes complete.

Dave Tyson Gentry

The first ingredient
in conversation
is truth;
the next, good sense;
the third, good humour;
the fourth,
wit.

Sir William Temple

'I can forgive but
I cannot forget,'

is only another
way of saying
'I cannot forgive'

Henry Ward Beecher

there are three kinds of friends:
Best friends,
Guest friends,
and Pest friends.

The anxiety of some people

to make new friends
is so intense
that they
never have
old
ones.

'WHEN YOU GET INTO A
TIGHT PLACE AND EVERYTHING
GOES AGAINST YOU, TILL IT SEEMS
AS THOUGH YOU COULD NOT HOLD
ON A MINUTE LONGER, NEVER GIVE
UP THEN, FOR THAT IS JUST THE
PLACE AND TIME THAT THE
TIDE WILL TURN.

Harriet Beecher Stowe

A FRIEND IS A PRESENT YOU GIVE YOURSELF.

Robert Louis Stevenson

It is possible to give without Loving,

but it is impossible to Love without giving.

LAUGHTER
IS THE SUN
THAT DRIVES
THE WINTER
FROM THE
HUMAN FACE

Victor Hugo

People are lonely because they build walls instead of bridges.

Joseph Fort Newton

You meet your
friend,
your face brightens~

you have struck
gold.

Kassia

Who ceases to be
a friend,
Never was one.

If the whole world
followed you ~

would it be
a better place?

The only rose
without thorns
is friendship

Madeline de Scudery

Lord, help me to be
a master of
myself
that I
may be
a servant
to others.

A real friend
never gets in your way,

unless you happen
to be on the way
down.

True friendship is like sound health,
the value of it is seldom known
until it is lost.

Charles Caleb Colton

spring
is a time when
youth dreams
and old age
remembers.

*Instead of loving
your enemies,
treat your friends
a little better.*

Ed Howe

Happy is the house
that shelters
a friend

Ralph Waldo Emerson

THERE ARE
THREE THINGS
THAT OUGHT TO BE
CONSIDERED BEFORE SOME THINGS
ARE SPOKEN;
THE MANNER,
THE PLACE
AND THE TIME.

One friend in
a lifetime is much; two
are many; three are
hardly possible.

Henry Adams

We make a living
by what we get,
but we make
a life
by what we give.

Winston Churchill

O LORD, FORGIVE US FOR
BEING SO SENSITIVE
ABOUT THINGS THAT
DO NOT MATTER —
AND SO INSENSITIVE
ABOUT THE THINGS
THAT DO.

amen.

IN PROSPERITY
OUR FRIENDS KNOW US;

IN ADVERSITY
WE KNOW OUR FRIENDS.

To like and dislike
the same things,
that is indeed
true friendship

Sallust 86~34 BC

friendships, like marriages, are dependent on avoiding the unforgivable.

John D. MacDonald

Do not save your loving speeches
For your friends till they are dead;
Do not write them on their tombstones,
Speak them rather now instead.

Anna Cummins

I don't like to commit
myself about
heaven & hell~
you see, I have
friends in both
places.

Mark Twain

Be slow in choosing a friend,
Slower in changing.

Benjamin Franklin

The seven modern sins

Policies without principles

Pleasure without conscience

Wealth without work

Knowledge without character

Industry without morality

Science without humanity

Worship without sacrifice

When I have lost my temper
I have lost my reason too,
I'm never proud of anything
Which angrily I do.

When I have walked in anger
And my cheeks are flaming red
I have always uttered something
That I wish I hadn't said.

In anger I have never done
A kindly deed, or wise,
But many things for which I know
I should apologize.

In looking back across my life
And all I've lost or made,
I can't recall a single time
When fury ever paid.

Life is not so much what each individual makes of it, but what we make of it for each other.

do not use
a hatchet
to remove
a fly
from
your friend's
forehead.

Chinese Proverb

*Shared joy is
double joy
and shared sorrow
is
half-sorrow.*

The truth that is
suppressed by friends
is the readiest weapon
of the enemy.

Robert Louis Stevenson.

Love without return
is like
a
question without
an answer.

I love you

not only
for what you are

but for what I am
when I'm
with you;

I love you
not only for what you
have made of yourself
but what
you are making of me;

You have done it
without a touch,
without a word,
without a sigh;

You have done it
by being yourself.

Perhaps that is what
being a friend means,
after all.

We do not inherit
the earth from
our ancestors,

we borrow it
from our
children.

Kenyan Proverb

never fear shadows.
They simply mean there's
a light shining
somewhere nearby.